HEARTFELT POSTURE

INTIMATE CONVERSATIONS WITH THE FATHER

KAMRYN MAKENZIE

COPYRIGHT © 2023 by KAMRYN MAKENZIE

All rights reserved. This book or any portion thereof may not be reproduced or used in any manner whatsoever without the express written permission of the publisher except for the use of brief quotations in a book review.

This book has been published with all reasonable efforts taken to make the material error-free after the consent of the author. No part of this book shall be used, reproduced in any manner whatsoever without written permission from the author, except in the case of brief quotations embodied in critical articles and reviews.

Scriptures marked NKJV are taken from the NEW KING JAMES VERSION (NKJV): Scripture taken from the NEW KING JAMES VERSION®. Copyright© 1982 by Thomas Nelson, Inc. Used by permission. All rights reserved.

Scriptures marked AMP are taken from the AMPLIFIED BIBLE (AMP): Scripture taken from the AMPLIFIED® BIBLE, Copyright © 1954, 1958, 1962, 1964, 1965, 1987 by the Lockman Foundation Used by Permission. (www.lockman.org)

Printed in the United States of America

ISBN 978-1-7359343-9-6 (Paperback)
ISBN 978-1-7359343-8-9 (E-Book)

DEDICATION

To my family, friends, and village of supporters, thank you for building me into a vigorous prayer warrior. I am forever grateful.

CONTENTS

ACKNOWLEDGMENTS vi
INTRODUCTION vii
Part I: Personal Prayers 1
   Confession of Faith 2
   Divine Guidance 3
   God Given Purpose 4
   The Anointing Oil 5
   Consecration 6
   Baptism of The Holy Spirit 7
   Family and Friends 8
   Prosperity and Health 9

Part II: Intercessions 10
   General Intercession 11
   World Crises 12
   Governmental Systems 13
   Salvation 14
   Revival 15
   Body of Christ 16
   Defeating Oppression 17
   Overcoming Depression & Anxiety 18
   The Economy 19

Part 3: Spiritual Warfare 20
Destroying Generational Curses 21
Breaking Strongholds 22
Rebuking Witchcraft 23
Releasing Blessings 24
Armor of God 25
Casting Out Demons 26
Renouncing New Age Practices 27
BIBLE PLAN 28
SCRIPTURE REFERENCES 50

ACKNOWLEDGMENTS

All praises to God Almighty for His goodness in helping me complete this divine assignment. Lord, I am forever grateful to be Your chosen vessel and stand in Your grace as a forgiven sinner. Thank You for being the TRUE author and finisher of this book.

I sincerely thank my parents, every pastor and spiritual leader who helped push me into purpose through persistent prayers and guidance. Each of you offered me a prototype of faith to live a life of Holy devotion to God. Thank you for your endurance as faithful leaders of His flock.

I want to express special thanks to my childhood best friend, Ladasha. Thank you for your consistent support and love over these past two decades. Our friendship is one I will always cherish. I pray that in every season, God would be your constant companion.

To those who buy and gift this book, thank you for extending hope, healing, and deliverance for the glory of God. Continue to push through every season, good or bad, one prayer at a time. May your testimonies build you into mighty, effective prayer warriors for the Kingdom. In Jesus' name.

With love,

Kamryn Makenzie

INTRODUCTION

Create in me a clean heart, O God, And renew a steadfast spirit within me.

— Psalms 51:10 NKJV

To tap into the spiritual realm, you need a ladder. A ladder is designed for escalation, helping you reach levels you cannot reach on your own. Prayer is the ladder of God. It is a direct communication to build a deeper relationship the Father and access hidden treasures. We should pray because we become intimate with whom, for whom, and to whom we pray.

So, what exactly is the posture of prayer? You may think of different stances such as standing, sitting, bowing, lifting hands, or lowering heads. While these visible positions are the most known within the church, they hold little to no significance without the most critical posture, the heart. Our hearts must continuously mirror our Savior, Jesus Christ, for our prayers to indeed be effective. Our prayers will lack substance if we enter the secret place with pride, bitterness, envy, jealousy, fear, and other fleshly attributes. We must make our personal pruning process a daily priority for both us and those we are called to minister to. If we do not concur self, we will be conquered by self. Purification will either come by choice or force.

This is the time to pursue the character and nature of God because prayer does not take place of the seed. Seeds grow from the inside out, not the outside in. When we draw near to Jesus Christ, we invite Him to change our lives. There is a crucial difference between Christ's invitation to come as you are and the unbiblical invitation to stay as you are. Nobody is going to change until they have a revelation of who He is.

This collection of heartfelt prayers guides Christians through personal and corporate healing, restoration, strength, and faith. When we pray through the agenda of heaven, we are assisting angels in doing God's will for the body of Christ. He rewards openly what we do in secret. Keep praying because when the prayers go up, the blessings come down.

PART I: PERSONAL PRAYERS

CONFESSION OF FAITH

Heavenly Father,

I humbly come before You, acknowledging that I am a sinner in need of Your saving grace. I confess my faith in Your Son, Jesus Christ, who is the Way, the Truth, and the Life. I believe that He died on the cross for my sins and rose again, victorious over death, so that I may have eternal life through Him.

Lord Jesus, I confess that I am lost without You. I surrender my life to You completely, placing my trust and hope in Your redemptive work. I acknowledge that Your blood cleanses me from all my sins and makes me a new creation in You. I confess that You are the Son of God, the Messiah, and my Savior. I believe that You have the power to transform my life, to heal my brokenness, and to give me hope and purpose. I declare that You are the Lord over every area of my life.

Thank You, Lord, for the gift of salvation and for the assurance of eternal life that I have through faith in Jesus Christ. May my life be a testimony of Your love and grace, shining brightly for all to see.

In Jesus' precious name, I pray. Amen.

SCRIPTURE REFERENCES
John 14:6 NKJV
1 John 1:7 NKJV
Romans 10:9 NKJV
Acts 3:19 NKJV
John 3:16 NKJV

DIVINE GUIDANCE

Dear Lord,

I come before You, seeking Your divine guidance and wisdom in every aspect of my life. You are the source of all wisdom and knowledge, and I trust in Your unfailing guidance to lead me on the right path. I surrender my plans and desires to You, knowing that Your plans for me are greater than anything I could ever imagine. I ask for clarity and discernment as I make decisions, big or small, knowing that You will guide me and show me the way.

Grant me the wisdom to seek Your will in all that I do, and the patience to wait for Your perfect timing. Help me to align my desires with Your purposes, so that my actions may bring glory to Your name. Holy Spirit, I invite You to lead and guide me, to speak to my heart and provide divine insight and understanding. Open my eyes to see the opportunities and challenges that lie before me and give me the courage to step out in faith, trusting in Your guidance.

Thank You, Father, for Your faithful guidance and for always being with me on this journey. I trust in Your unfailing love and know that as I seek Your guidance, You will lead me into a life that is pleasing to You. In Jesus' precious name, I pray. Amen.

SCRIPTURE REFERENCES
Psalm 48:14 NKJV
Proverbs 19:21 NKJV
John 16:13 NKJV
Matthew 6:33 NKJV

GOD GIVEN PURPOSE

Heavenly Father,

I come before You today seeking clarity and guidance as I search for my purpose in life. You have created me with unique gifts, talents, and passions, and I desire to use them in a way that brings honor to Your name. I surrender my own plans and ambitions to You, knowing that Your purpose for my life far surpasses anything I could imagine.

Open my eyes to recognize the opportunities and doors that You place before me. Grant me wisdom and discernment as I make choices that align with Your purposes. As I navigate through life, may Your Holy Spirit be my constant companion, leading me in the way I should go.

Lord, I surrender my plans, dreams, and ambitions to You. Align my heart with Yours and mold me into the person You have created me to be. May my life reflect Your love and grace, impacting those around me for Your kingdom's sake. Grant me the courage to step out in faith and live a life of purpose, wholly surrendered to You.

I pray all these things in the precious name of Jesus. Amen.

SCRIPTURE REFERENCES
Philippians 1:6 AMP
Psalm 139:13-14 AMP
Jeremiah 29:11 AMP

THE ANOINTING OIL

Gracious Father,

As I prepare to use this oil for a sacred purpose, I ask that You infuse it with Your power, Your healing, and Your blessings. May it become a tangible representation of Your love and grace in my life. Lord, I recognize the significance of anointing oil as a symbol of Your healing and restoration. I ask that as I apply this oil, You would touch every aspect of my being, bringing forth wholeness and restoration according to Your perfect will.

I pray that this oil would refresh and invigorate my mind, my thoughts, and my spirit. May it overflow with Your divine favor and blessings, even amid challenges and opposition. I ask that as I apply this oil, any burdens, yokes, or chains that may be weighing me down will be broken and destroyed in the mighty name of Jesus. Grant me freedom and release from every bondage and limitation. May this serve as a reminder of the indwelling Holy Spirit within me, teaching me, guiding me, and illuminating Your truth in my life.

I consecrate this oil for Your purposes. May it be a symbol of Your presence, a catalyst for Your power, and a testimony of Your faithfulness. I receive Your anointing upon my life and declare that I am set apart for Your divine purposes.
In the precious name of Jesus, I pray. Amen.

SCRIPTURE REFERENCES
James 5:14 AMP
Psalm 23:5 AMP
1 John 2:27 AMP

CONSECRATION

Heavenly Father,

I bow before You in reverence and awe, recognizing Your holiness and majesty. I come before You today to consecrate myself wholly to You. I surrender my heart, my mind, my body, and my soul into Your loving hands.

Lord, I desire to live a life that is set apart for Your purposes. Your Word reminds me that I am to present my body as a living sacrifice, holy and well-pleasing to You, which is my reasonable and logical service of worship. I offer myself to You as a living sacrifice, surrendering my will and my desires to Your perfect will.

Lord, I consecrate my thoughts and my mind to You. Help me to think on things that are true, noble, just, pure, lovely, of good report, virtuous, and praiseworthy, as Your Word instructs. Lord, I consecrate my actions and my behavior to You. Help me to walk in integrity and righteousness, reflecting Your character in all that I do.

Guide me by Your Holy Spirit and empower me to live a life that is pleasing to You, bearing the fruit of the Spirit: love, joy, peace, patience, kindness, goodness, faithfulness, gentleness, and self-control. In Jesus' name, Amen!

SCRIPTURE REFERENCES
Romans 12:1 AMP
Philippians 4:8 AMP
Galatians 5:22-23 AMP

Heartfelt Posture

BAPTISM OF THE HOLY SPIRIT

Gracious Heavenly Father,

I come before Your presence, seeking the precious gift of the baptism of the Holy Spirit and the manifestation of speaking in tongues. Your Word assures me that this gift is available to all who believe and ask in faith. I long to experience a deeper intimacy with You and a greater empowerment for Your Kingdom purposes.

Holy Spirit, I invite You to come and fill me to overflowing. I ask for the baptism of Your Spirit, that I may be immersed in Your presence and power. I desire to be clothed with Your authority, equipped for the work You have called me to do.

As I receive the baptism of the Holy Spirit, I ask for a greater measure of Your fruit to be evident in my life. Fill me with love, joy, peace, patience, kindness, goodness, faithfulness, gentleness, and self-control. Let these qualities overflow from my heart and impact those I encounter.

Thank You, Lord, for hearing my prayer. I trust that You will fulfill Your promises to those who seek You. I yield myself to Your Spirit's leading, and I eagerly anticipate the transformation and empowerment that the baptism of the Holy Spirit brings. In the mighty name of Jesus, I pray. Amen.

SCRIPTURE REFERENCES
Luke 11:13 AMP
Acts 2:4 AMP
Luke 24:49 NKJV

FAMILY AND FRIENDS

Heavenly Father,

I lift my family and friends in prayer. I thank You for the precious gift of their presence in my life, and I ask for Your loving guidance and protection over each one of them.

Lord, I pray that You would strengthen the bonds of love and unity within our families and friendships. Help us to be a source of encouragement, support, and inspiration to one another. May our relationships be built on trust, forgiveness, and understanding, reflecting Your unconditional love for us.

Father, I also pray for the spiritual growth of my family and friends. May Your Word be a lamp unto our feet and a light unto our path. Help us to hunger and thirst for righteousness and to grow in our knowledge and understanding of You. May our lives be a testimony of Your grace and truth.

Finally, Lord, I ask for Your blessings and favor to be upon my family and friends. Open doors of opportunity, guide their steps, and fulfill the desires of their hearts according to Your will. May we always acknowledge You as the source of our blessings and give You thanks for Your goodness and faithfulness.

In the name of Jesus, I pray. Amen.

SCRIPTURE REFERENCES
Psalm 119:105 NKJV
Matthew 5:6 NKJV
Psalm 46:1 NKJV

PROSPERITY AND HEALTH

Gracious Lord,

I humbly come before You, seeking Your abundant blessings of prosperity and health. You are the source of all good things, and I acknowledge that every good and perfect gift comes from You. I thank You for the blessings You have already bestowed upon me, and I ask for Your continued favor in my life.

Father, I pray for prosperity in every area of my life. Guide me in my endeavors and grant me wisdom to make sound decisions. Open doors of opportunity and bless the work of my hands. May my financial resources be used to honor You and bless others. Help me to be a good steward of the blessings You entrust to me.

Lord, I also lift up my health before You. You are the Great Physician, and I ask for Your healing touch upon my body. Strengthen my immune system and protect me from illness and disease. Grant me vitality, energy, and good health to serve You and fulfill my purpose. Help me to make healthy choices and care for my body, which is Your temple.

Thank You, Lord, for hearing my prayer. I trust in Your faithfulness and provision. May Your name be glorified through the prosperity and good health You bestow upon me. In Jesus' name, I pray. Amen.

SCRIPTURE REFERENCES
James 1:17 NKJV
1 Corinthians 6:19-20 NKJV

Part II: Intercessions

Heartfelt Posture

GENERAL INTERCESSION

Heavenly Father,

In Your infinite love and mercy, we lift our intercessory prayers before You, knowing that You are attentive to our every need. We come before Your throne, humbly seeking Your guidance, provision, and protection. We base our prayers on the unchanging truth of Your Word.

Father, we pray for unity and love to prevail among Your people. Help us to love one another as Christ loved us. Remove any divisions, prejudices, or selfishness that hinder our unity. May our love and unity be a powerful testimony to the world of our relationship with You.

Lord, we desire to grow in our relationship with You. We ask for an increase in faith, wisdom, and understanding of Your Word. Transform us by the power of Your Holy Spirit and conform us into the image of Christ. Help us to bear fruit that brings glory to Your name.

In Jesus' name, we pray, amen.

SCRIPTURE REFERENCES
2 Peter 3:18 NKJV
John 13:34-35 NKJV

WORLD CRISES

Gracious and merciful Father,

We come before You with heavy hearts, burdened by the crises that plague our world. We acknowledge Your sovereignty and power, knowing that You are able to bring hope, healing, and restoration even in the midst of chaos. We intercede on behalf of our world, seeking Your intervention and guidance. As we pray, we cling to the promises of Your Word.

Father, we cry out for justice in a world plagued by oppression, inequality, and injustice. Strengthen those who champion righteousness and advocate for the marginalized and oppressed. Bring forth systemic change and eradicate corruption. May justice flow like a mighty river, bringing restoration and healing to the broken.

Father, in the face of despair and hopelessness, we cling to the hope found in You. Fill hearts with Your joy and peace, even in the midst of chaos and uncertainty. Let hope arise, inspiring courage, resilience, and perseverance. May Your hope shine brightly, drawing people to You.

We trust in Your unfailing love and mercy, knowing that You are able to bring beauty out of ashes. May Your kingdom come, and Your will be done on earth as it is in heaven.

In Jesus' name, we pray, amen.

SCRIPTURE REFERENCES
Romans 15:13 NKJV
Micah 6:8 NKJV

Heartfelt Posture

GOVERNMENTAL SYSTEMS

Gracious and Sovereign God,

We come before You today, lifting the governmental systems of our world. We recognize that You are the ultimate authority and that all earthly authorities are established by Your divine providence. We intercede on behalf of these systems, seeking Your wisdom, guidance, and righteousness to prevail. As we pray, we anchor our supplications in the truth of Your Word.

Lord, we lift up our leaders before You. Grant them wisdom, discernment, and integrity in their decision-making. May they govern with justice, compassion, and a heart for the well-being of all citizens. We ask that You surround them with wise counselors who will offer godly advice and guide them in righteousness.

Heavenly Father, we ask for leaders who govern with humility, integrity, and a reverence for You. Raise up men and women of character who prioritize the common good over personal gain. Give them discernment to make sound decisions, compassion to address the needs of the vulnerable, and a commitment to uphold truth and righteousness.

In all things, we acknowledge Your sovereignty and trust in Your perfect plan. May Your will be done in the governments of our world as it is in heaven.

In the name of Jesus, our ultimate King, we pray, amen.

SCRIPTURE REFERENCES
Psalm 33:12 AMP
Proverbs 14:34 AMP
1 Timothy 2:1-2 AMP

SALVATION

Heavenly Father,

We come before You with humble hearts, seeking Your mercy and grace for the salvation of our loved ones and all those who are lost and in need of Your saving power.

Lord, we lift [mention the names of individuals] to Your loving care. We ask that You draw them to Yourself, soften their hearts, and open their minds to the truth of Your Word. Help them to see their need for a Savior and the hope that can only be found in Jesus Christ.

Lord, we pray for divine encounters and opportunities for these dear ones to hear and receive the Gospel message. Send laborers into their lives, whether it be family, friends, coworkers, or even strangers, who will speak the truth of Your Word with love and conviction.

Father, we know that salvation is a work of Your Spirit, so we pray for the Holy Spirit to convict their hearts of sin, righteousness, and judgment. Soften their hearts, break the chains of sin that bind them, and give them a deep desire to repent and turn to You.

We eagerly await the day when these dear ones will experience the joy of salvation and become part of Your eternal family.

In the mighty name of Jesus, we pray. Amen.

SCRIPTURE REFERENCES
Acts 4:12 NKJV
Romans 10:13 AMP

REVIVAL

Heavenly Father,

We acknowledge that revival begins in the hearts of individuals. We ask for a stirring of Your Spirit within each person, awakening a hunger and thirst for righteousness. Remove complacency and spiritual apathy and ignite a passion for You and Your Word.

We pray for unity among believers, transcending denominational and cultural barriers. Unite us in a common purpose to advance Your kingdom and share the Good News with the world. Remove any divisions, envy, and strife, and replace them with love, compassion, and a heart for evangelism.

Lord, we believe that You can do immeasurably more than we can ask or imagine. We trust in Your promises and hold on to the hope that You will bring about a global revival that will usher in a spiritual awakening unlike anything we have ever seen.

In the mighty name of Jesus, we pray. Amen.

SCRIPTURE REFERENCES
Psalm 85:6 AMP
Psalm 80:19 AMP

BODY OF CHRIST

Heavenly Father,

We come before You as members of the body of Christ, Your Church, united by our faith in Your Son, Jesus Christ. We lift up the Church to You, interceding for its growth, unity, and spiritual vitality. We believe that You have called us to be Your ambassadors and instruments of Your love and grace in the world.

Lord, we pray for the Church to arise in power and influence in these times. Strengthen Your Church with a deep love for You and a passion for Your Word. May Your truth be proclaimed boldly and faithfully, guiding, and directing the steps of Your people.

We lift up persecuted believers around the world. Strengthen and sustain them in the face of opposition and persecution. Grant them courage, wisdom, and endurance to stand firm in their faith, even amid trials. Surround them with Your supernatural protection and comfort them with Your presence.

May Your Church be a beacon of hope, shining Your light in a dark world and drawing people to Yourself. In the name of Jesus, we pray. Amen.

SCRIPTURE REFERENCES
Psalm 85:6 NKJV
Psalm 80:19 NKJV

DEFEATING OPPRESSION

Dear Lord,

We declare Your power and authority over every force of darkness that seeks to oppress and subjugate. We rebuke the spirit of oppression and command it to release its hold on us and on those who are suffering. We ask that You expose the systems of injustice and bring about a transformation that leads to freedom, equality, and dignity for all.

Lord, we pray for strength and courage for those who are oppressed. Grant them resilience in the face of adversity and the ability to rise above their circumstances. Surround them with Your love and protection and provide them with the necessary resources and support they need to overcome oppression. May they find solace in Your presence and be filled with hope for a better tomorrow.

We also pray for those who perpetrate oppression. Soften their hearts and open their eyes to the pain and suffering they inflict upon others. Help them to recognize the inherent worth and value of every human being and lead them to repentance and a change of heart. May they become instruments of justice, reconciliation, and healing in our world.

In Jesus name, Amen.

SCRIPTURE REFERENCES
James 1:27 NKJV
Psalm 9:9 NKJV

OVERCOMING DEPRESSION & ANXIETY

Dear Lord,

In the name of Jesus, we break every chain of darkness and negativity that seeks to keep us captive. We declare Your power and authority over our lives, knowing that You have promised to give us a future and a hope. Help us to cast our burdens upon You, for You care for us deeply. Lift the heaviness from our hearts and minds and replace it with Your perfect peace that surpasses all understanding.

Lord, we pray for clarity of thought and renewed strength. Fill our minds with Your truth and help us to focus on the things that are good, noble, and praiseworthy. We ask that You guide us to seek help when needed, whether it be through therapy, counseling, or medical intervention. Grant us the wisdom to make the right choices for our well-being and surround us with understanding and supportive people.

We also pray for resilience in our journey. Help us to persevere through the darkest moments, knowing that You are with us every step of the way. We surrender our anxieties and fears to You, knowing that You are our refuge and fortress. Fill us with Your joy, peace, and hope, and help us to walk in the freedom that You have promised us. In the mighty name of Jesus, we pray, believing that You can overcome all things. Amen.

SCRIPTURE REFERENCES
Matthew 11:28-30 NKJV
Psalm 34:17-18 AMP

THE ECONOMY

Heavenly Father,

We come before You today with concerns and prayers for our economy. We acknowledge that You are the ultimate provider and sustainer of all things, including the economic well-being of nations and individuals. We humbly ask for Your guidance, wisdom, and intervention in the economic challenges we face.

We ask for integrity, transparency, and accountability in all financial matters. Help us to prioritize the well-being of all individuals, especially the vulnerable and marginalized, in our economic policies and decisions.

Lord, we pray for those who are struggling financially. Provide for their needs and grant them the strength and resilience to persevere in difficult times. Open doors of opportunity, employment, and provision for those who are seeking livelihoods. We ask for creativity and innovation to flourish, leading to economic growth and stability. Help us to be good stewards of the resources You have blessed us with, using them to bless others and bring about positive change.

In the mighty name of Jesus, we pray, believing that You are the provider and sustainer of all things, including our economy. Amen.

SCRIPTURE REFERENCES
Philippians 4:19 NKJV
Proverbs 3:9-10 NKJV

Part 3: Spiritual Warfare

DESTROYING GENERATIONAL CURSES

Heavenly Father, Creator of all things, I humbly come before Your presence, seeking Your mercy and grace. Lord, I acknowledge that as descendants of Adam, we are all prone to the effects of sin and its consequences. I repent on behalf of myself and my ancestors, recognizing that we have strayed from Your perfect will and brought generational curses upon our lives.

I declare that I am a new creation in Christ Jesus. Through His blood shed on the cross, I am redeemed from the power of the curse. I renounce and break every curse that has affected my family line, in the name of Jesus.

Father, I invite Your Holy Spirit to cleanse and purify every aspect of my life that has been tainted by these curses. I release forgiveness for those who have wronged us in the past, and I choose to walk in obedience to Your commandments. Lord, I pray that Your divine protection, favor, and blessings will flow freely through our family line from this moment onward.

Thank You, gracious Lord, for Your love and faithfulness. I trust in Your promises, and I believe that as I surrender to Your will, You will transform generational curses into generational blessings. In the mighty and precious name of Jesus, I pray. Amen.

SCRIPTURE REFERENCES
Exodus 20:5; NKJV
Exodus 34:7 AMP
Galatians 3:13-14 NKJV

BREAKING STRONGHOLDS

Almighty God, Sovereign King, I approach Your throne with reverence and awe, recognizing Your supreme authority over all creation. Lord, I bring before You the strongholds that have taken root in my life and hindered my spiritual growth and intimacy with You. Your Word declares in 2 Corinthians 10:4-5 that the weapons of our warfare are not carnal, but mighty in You for pulling down strongholds.

Heavenly Father, I acknowledge that these strongholds have arisen from wrong thought patterns, past wounds, and ungodly influences. I repent for entertaining thoughts and behaviors that are contrary to Your truth. I renounce and break the power of every stronghold that has held me captive. I release forgiveness to those who have hurt me and extend grace to myself for my own shortcomings.

Lord, fill me with Your Spirit and Your Word. Strengthen me to walk in the freedom that Christ has secured for me. I ask for the power to resist temptation and to stand firm against the schemes of the enemy. I believe that as I continue to abide in You, these strongholds will crumble, and I will experience the fullness of life that You have promised. In Jesus' powerful name, I pray. Amen.

SCRIPTURE REFERENCES
2 Corinthians 10:4-5 AMP
2 Corinthians 4:4 NKJV

REBUKING WITCHCRAFT

Eternal God, who reigns over all creation, I bow before You, acknowledging Your limitless power and unwavering protection. Heavenly Father, I am aware of the spiritual battles that rage unseen, and I come before You to rebuke and nullify any form of witchcraft or dark influence that seeks to harm or hinder me.

In the authority of Jesus Christ, my Savior and Redeemer, I declare that I am covered by the blood of the Lamb. Your Word in Isaiah 54:17 assures me that no weapon formed against me shall prosper, and every tongue that rises against me in judgment, I shall condemn. I take hold of this promise and affirm that I am shielded by Your divine authority.

Lord, I rebuke and bind any curses, hexes, spells, or evil intentions that may have been directed toward me or my loved ones. I reject fear and stand firm in faith, for greater is He who is in me than he who is in the world. I invoke the power of Your angels to surround me, guarding and protecting me from all spiritual harm.

Father, shine Your light into the darkness, exposing the works of the enemy. Illuminate my path with Your truth and guide me into all wisdom. As I dwell in Your presence, I am confident that no enchantment or divination can prevail against me. I trust in Your unfailing love and declare victory over all forces of darkness, in the matchless name of Jesus. Amen.

SCRIPTURE REFERENCES
Isaiah 41:10 NKJV
1 John 4:4 AMP

RELEASING BLESSINGS

Gracious Father,

I come before You with a heart overflowing with gratitude and expectation. Your Word in Deuteronomy 28:2 declares that all blessings shall come upon me and overtake me when I heed Your voice and obey Your commandments. Lord, I desire to walk in alignment with Your will and experience the fullness of Your blessings.

Heavenly Father, I invite Your Holy Spirit to guide my steps and direct my decisions. Help me to discern Your will and to live a life that honors You. I ask for Your wisdom and favor in my relationships, my work, my finances, and my health. May Your blessings overflow from my life and touch the lives of others.

Lord, I commit to using the blessings You bestow upon me to bless others and to advance Your kingdom. As I steward Your blessings faithfully, may Your name be glorified, and may Your light shine through me. Thank You for Your unending love and provision. I receive Your blessings with a grateful heart, in the name of Jesus. Amen.

SCRIPTURE REFERENCES
Deuteronomy 28:2 NKJV
Psalm 31:1-3 AMP

ARMOR OF GOD

Heavenly Father, today, I humbly clothe myself with the spiritual armor You provide, equipping me to face the challenges and battles that come my way. Your Word teaches me in Ephesians 6:10-18 that my struggle is not against flesh and blood, but against principalities, against powers, against the rulers of the darkness of this age, against spiritual hosts of wickedness in the heavenly places. As I put on each piece of the armor, I do so with intention and faith, knowing that in Your strength, I am more than a conqueror.

Lord, I fasten the belt of truth around my waist. I put on the breastplate of righteousness to guard my heart. I lace up the shoes of peace, prepared to walk in Your ways and share the Gospel of peace wherever I go. I take up the shield of faith, which can extinguish all the enemy's fiery darts. I place the helmet of salvation upon my head, guarding my mind and thoughts.

In my hand, I hold the sword of the Spirit, which is the Word of God. I recognize that my strength comes from You alone. Grant me the wisdom to pray without ceasing, seeking Your guidance and power in every circumstance. Thank you, Lord, for arming me with the tools I need to stand firm against the forces of darkness. In Jesus' mighty name, I pray. Amen.

SCRIPTURE REFERENCES
Ephesians 6:14-18 NKJV

Heartfelt Posture

CASTING OUT DEMONS

Heavenly Father, I come before Your throne of grace with a heart filled with faith and determination. Your Word assures me that in the name of Jesus, I have authority over all the powers of darkness (Luke 10:19). Today, I stand on this promise as I engage in spiritual warfare to cast out any demons that may be afflicting and oppressing.

In the name of Jesus Christ, the Savior and Redeemer, I rebuke and command every unclean spirit, every demonic presence, and every stronghold to flee from the lives of those affected by their influence. I declare that the power of the Cross has already defeated the enemy, and I claim victory in Jesus' name.

I declare that the power of the Holy Spirit breaks every argument, deception, and stronghold of the enemy. I bring every thought, emotion, and influence into captivity to the obedience of Christ. I release the truth and light of God's Word to expose and defeat the darkness.

Thank you, Lord, for granting me the authority to cast out demons and to set captives free. I unite with fellow believers, interceding for the deliverance and healing of those in need. May Your name be glorified through the liberation of souls from the clutches of darkness. In the mighty and victorious name of Jesus, I pray. Amen.

SCRIPTURE REFERENCES
Matthew 10:8 NKJV
Mark 16:17 AMP

RENOUNCING NEW AGE PRACTICES

Heavenly Father, I come before You with a repentant heart, acknowledging any involvement I have had in occult and new age practices. I confess that these actions have taken me away from the purity and truth of Your Word, and I now choose to turn away from them and seek Your forgiveness and cleansing.

Lord, Your Word warns us against any form of divination, witchcraft, or consulting with familiar spirits in Deuteronomy 18:10-12. I renounce and reject any association with these practices, and I ask for Your forgiveness for allowing myself to be ensnared by their deceit.

I choose to embrace You, the One True God, and to seek Your wisdom, guidance, and revelation through prayer, worship, and the study of Your Word. I commit to walking in the light of Your truth, renouncing all darkness and deception that once held sway over my life.

In the name of Jesus, I break every soul tie and connection with occult practices, declaring that my allegiance is to Christ alone. I declare my complete surrender to You, Lord, and I ask that You cleanse me, renew me, and set me free from the snares of the enemy.

SCRIPTURE REFERENCES
1 John 1:9 NKJV
Psalm 119:9-11 AMP

BIBLE PLAN

Using a weekly Bible reading plan alongside a collection of prayers creates a beautiful rhythm of connecting with God through both spoken and written words. It invites you to engage in a conversation with the Creator, drawing closer to Him and allowing Him to speak to your heart through His Word.

Week 1

Gen 1-3

Gen 4-6

Gen 7-9

Gen 10-13

Gen 14-16

Gen 17-19

Week 2

Gen 20-22

Gen 23-26

Gen 27-29

Gen 30-32

Gen 33-35

Gen 36-39

Gen 40-42

Week 3

Gen 43-45

Gen 46-48

Gen 49-50; Ex 1-2

Ex 3-5

Ex 6-8

Ex 9-11

Ex 12-15

Week 4

Ex 16-18

Ex 19-21

Ex 22-24

Ex 25-28

Ex 29-31

Ex 32-34

Ex 35-37

Week 5

Ex 38-40; Lev 1

Lev 2-4

Lev 5-7

Lev 8-10

Lev 11-14

Lev 15-17

Lev 18-20

Week 6

Lev 21-24

Lev 25-27

Num 1-3

Num 4-6

Num 7-10

Num 11-13

Num 14-16

Week 7

Num 17-19

Num 20-23

Num 24-26

Num 27-29

Num 30-32

Num 33-36

Deut 1-3

Week 8

Deut 4-6

Deut 7-9

Deut 10-13

Deut 14-16

Deut 17-19

Deut 20-22

Deut 23-26

Week 9

Deut 27-29

Deut 30-32

Deut 33-34; Josh 1

Josh 2-5

Josh 6-8

Josh 9-11

Josh 12-14

Week 10

Josh 15-18

Josh 19-21

Josh 22-24

Jdg 1-3

Jdg 4-7

Jdg 8-10

Jdg 11-13

Week 11

Jdg 14-17

Jdg 18-20

Jdg 21; Rut 1-2

Rut 3-4; 1 Sa 1

1 Sa 2-5

1 Sa 6-8

1 Sa 9-11

Week 12

1 Sa 12-14

1 Sa 15-18

1 Sa 19-21

1 Sa 22-24

1 Sa 25-27

1 Sa 28-31

2 Sa 1-3

Week 13

2 Sa 4-6

2 Sa 7-9

2 Sa 10-13

2 Sa 14-16

2 Sa 17-19

2 Sa 20-22

2 Sa 23-24; 1 Kgs 1-2

Week 14

1 Kgs 3-5

1 Kgs 6-8

1 Kgs 9-11

1 Kgs 12-15

1 Kgs 16-18

1 Kgs 19-21

1 Kgs 22; 2 Kgs 1-2

Week 15

2 Kgs 3-6

2 Kgs 7-9

2 Kgs 10-12

2 Kgs 13-16

2 Kgs 17-19

2 Kgs 20-22

2 Kgs 23-25

Week 16

1 Chr 1-4

1 Chr 5-7

1 Chr 8-10

1 Chr 11-13

1 Chr 14-17

1 Chr 18-20

1 Chr 21-23

Week 17

1 Chr 24-26

1 Chr 27-29; 2 Chr 1

2 Chr 2-4

2 Chr 5-7

2 Chr 8-10

2 Chr 11-14

2 Chr 15-17

Week 18

2 Chr 18-20

2 Chr 21-23

2 Chr 24-27

2 Chr 28-30

2 Chr 31-33

2 Chr 34-36

Ezr 1-4

Week 19

Ezr 5-7

Ezr 8-10

Neh 1-3

Neh 4-7

Neh 8-10

Neh 11-13

Est 1-3

Week 20

Est 4-7

Est 8-10

Job 1-3

Job 4-7

Job 8-10

Job 11-13

Job 14-16

Week 21

Job 17-20

Job 21-23

Job 24-26

Job 27-29

Job 30-33

Job 34-36

Job 37-39

Week 22

Job 40-42

Ps 1-4

Ps 5-7

Ps 8-10

Ps 11-13

Ps 14-17

Ps 18-20

Week 23

Ps 21-23

Ps 24-26

Ps 27-30

Ps 31-33

Ps 34-36

Ps 37-39

Ps 40-43

Week 24

Ps 44-46

Ps 47-49

Ps 50-52

Ps 53-56

Ps 57-59

Ps 60-62

Ps 63-66

Week 25

Ps 67-69

Ps 70-72

Ps 73-75

Ps 76-79

Ps 80-82

Ps 83-85

Ps 86-88

Week 26

Ps 89-92

Ps 93-95

Ps 96-98

Ps 99-101

Ps 102-105

Ps 106-108

Ps 109-111

Week 27

Ps 112-114

Ps 115-118

Ps 119-121

Ps 122-124

Ps 125-127

Ps 128-131

Ps 132-134

Week 28

Ps 135-137

Ps 138-140

Ps 141-144

Ps 145-147

Ps 148-150

Pro 1-3

Pro 4-7

Week 29

Pro 8-10

Pro 11-13

Pro 14-16

Pro 17-20

Pro 21-23

Pro 24-26

Pro 27-30

Week 30

Pro 31; Ecc 1-2

Ecc 3-5

Ecc 6-8

Ecc 9-12

Sos 1-3

Sos 4-6

Sos 7-8; Isa 1

Week 31

Isa 2-5

Isa 6-8

Isa 9-11

Isa 12-14

Isa 15-18

Isa 19-21

Isa 22-24

Week 32

Isa 25-27

Isa 28-31

Isa 32-34

Isa 35-37

Isa 38-40

Isa 41-44

Isa 45-47

Week 33

Isa 48-50

Isa 51-53

Isa 54-57

Isa 58-60

Isa 61-63

Isa 64-66

Jer 1-4

Week 34

Jer 5-7

Jer 8-10

Jer 11-14

Jer 15-17

Jer 18-20

Jer 21-23

Jer 24-27

Week 35

Jer 28-30

Jer 31-33

Jer 34-36

Jer 37-40

Jer 41-43

Jer 44-46

Jer 47-49

Week 36

Jer 50-52; Lam 1

Lam 2-4

Lam 5; Eze 1-2

Eze 3-5

Eze 6-9

Eze 10-12

Eze 13-15

Week 37

Eze 16-18

Eze 19-22

Eze 23-25

Eze 26-28

Eze 29-31

Eze 32-35

Eze 36-38

Week 38

Eze 39-41

Eze 42-44

Eze 45-48

Dan 1-3

Dan 4-6

Dan 7-9

Dan 10-12; Hos 1

Week 39

Hos 2-4

Hos 5-7

Hos 8-11

Hos 12-14

Joe 1-3

Amo 1-3

Amo 4-7

Week 40

Amo 8-9; Oba

Jon 1-3

Jon 4; Mic 1-2

Mic 3-6

Mic 7; Nah 1-2

Nah 3; Hab 1-2

Hab 3; Zep 1-2

Week 41

Zep 3; Hag 1-2; Zec 1

Zec 2-4

Zec 5-7

Zec 8-10

Zec 11-14

Mal 1-3

Mal 4; Mat 1-2

Week 42

Mat 3-5

Mat 6-9

Mat 10-12

Mat 13-15

Mat 16-18

Mat 19-22

Mat 23-25

Week 43

Mat 26-28

Mk 1-3

Mk 4-7

Mk 8-10

Mk 11-13

Mk 14-16; Luk 1

Luk 2-4

Week 44

Luk 5-7

Luk 8-10

Luk 11-14

Luk 15-17

Luk 18-20

Luk 21-23

Luk 24; John 1-3

Week 45

John 4-6

John 7-9

John 10-12

John 13-16

John 17-19

John 20-21; Acts 1

Acts 2-4

Week 46

Acts 5-8

Acts 9-11

Acts 12-14

Acts 15-17

Acts 18-21

Acts 22-24

Acts 25-27

Week 47

Acts 28; Rom 1-2

Rom 3-6

Rom 7-9

Rom 10-12

Rom 13-15

Rom 16; 1 Co 1-3

1 Co 4-6

Week 48

1 Co 7-9

1 Co 10-12

1 Co 13-16

2 Co 1-3

2 Co 4-6

2 Co 7-10

2 Co 11-13

Week 49

Gal 1-3

Gal 4-6

Eph 1-4

Eph 5-6; Phil 1

Phil 2-4

Col 1-3

Col 4; 1 Th 1-3

Week 50

1 Th 4-5; 2 Th 1

2 Th 2-3; 1 Ti 1

1 Ti 2-4

1 Ti 5-6; 2 Ti 1-2

2 Ti 3-4; Tit 1

Tit 2-3; Phlm

Heb 1-3

Week 51

Heb 4-7

Heb 8-10

Heb 11-13

Jam 1-3

Jam 4-5; 1 Pe 1-2

1 Pe 3-5

2 Pe 1-3

Week 52

1 Jn 1-3

1 Jn 4-5; 2 Jn; 3 Jn

Jude; Rev 1-2

Rev 3-5

Rev 6-8

Rev 9-12

Rev 13-15

Week 53

Rev 16-18

Rev 19-22

SCRIPTURE REFERENCES

Exodus 20:5 NKJV- "You shall not bow down to them nor serve them. For I, the LORD your God, am a jealous God, visiting the iniquity of the fathers upon the children to the third and fourth generations of those who hate Me."

Exodus 34:7 AMP - "Keeping mercy and lovingkindness for thousands, forgiving iniquity and transgression and sin, but Who will by no means clear the guilty, visiting the iniquity of the fathers upon the children and the children's children, to the third and fourth generation."

Deuteronomy 28:2 NKJV - "And all these blessings shall come upon you and overtake you, because you obey the voice of the LORD your God."

Psalm 9:9 NKJV - "The LORD also will be a refuge for the oppressed, a refuge in times of trouble."

Psalm 23:5 AMP - "You prepare a table before me in the presence of my enemies. You anoint my head with oil; my [brimming] cup runs over."

Psalm 31:1-3 AMP - "In You, O LORD, I have placed my trust and taken refuge; let me never be ashamed; in Your righteousness deliver me. Bow down Your ear to me, deliver me speedily; be my rock of refuge, a strong fortress to save me! Yes, You are my rock and my fortress; for Your name's sake lead me and guide me."

Psalm 33:12 AMP - "Blessed [fortunate, prosperous, and favored by God] is the nation whose God is the LORD, the people whom He has chosen as His inheritance."

Psalm 34:17-18 AMP - "The righteous cry [out for help], and the LORD hears [and delivers them] and rescues them from all their distress and troubles. The LORD is near to the heartbroken and He saves those who are crushed in spirit (contrite in heart, truly sorry for their sin)."

Psalm 46:1 NKJV - "God is our refuge and strength, a very present help in trouble."

Psalm 48:14 NKJV - "For this is God, our God forever and ever; He will be our guide even to death."

Psalm 80:19 AMP - "Restore us, O LORD God of hosts; cause Your face to shine on us [in favor and approval], and we shall be saved."

Psalm 80:19 NKJV - "Restore us, O LORD God of hosts; cause Your face to shine, and we shall be saved!"

Psalm 85:6 AMP - "Will You not revive us and bring us to life again, that Your people may rejoice in You?"

Psalm 85:6 NKJV - "Will You not revive us again, that Your people may rejoice in You?"

Psalm 119:9-11 AMP -"How can a young man keep his way pure? By keeping watch [on himself] according to Your word [conforming his life to Your precepts]. With all my heart I have sought You, [inquiring of You and longing for You]; Do not let me wander from Your commandments [neither through ignorance nor by willful disobedience]. Your word I have treasured and stored in my heart, that I may not sin against You."

Psalm 119:105 NKJV - "Your word is a lamp to my feet and a light to my path."

Proverbs 3:9-10 NKJV - "Honor the LORD with your possessions, and with the firstfruits of all your increase; so your barns will be filled with plenty, and your vats will overflow with new wine."

Proverbs 14:34 AMP - "Righteousness [moral and spiritual integrity and virtuous character] exalts a nation, but sin is a disgrace to any people."

Proverbs 19:21 NKJV - "There are many plans in a man's heart, nevertheless the LORD's counsel—that will stand."

Isaiah 41:10 NKJV - "Fear not, for I am with you; be not dismayed, for I am your God. I will strengthen you, yes, I will help you, I will uphold you with My righteous right hand."

Jeremiah 29:11 AMP - "'For I know the plans and thoughts that I have for you,' says the LORD, 'plans for peace and well-being and not for disaster, to give you a future and a hope.'"

Micah 6:8 NKJV - "He has shown you, O man, what is good; and what does the LORD require of you but to do justly, to love mercy, and to walk humbly with your God?"

Matthew 5:6 NKJV - "Blessed are those who hunger and thirst for righteousness, for they shall be filled."

Matthew 6:33 NKJV - "But seek first the kingdom of God and His righteousness, and all these things shall be added to you."

Matthew 10:8 NKJV - "Heal the sick, cleanse the lepers, raise the dead, cast out demons. Freely you have received, freely give."

Matthew 11:28-30 NKJV - "Come to Me, all you who labor and are heavy laden, and I will give you rest. Take My yoke upon you and learn from Me, for I am gentle and lowly in heart, and you will find rest for your souls. For My yoke is easy and My burden is light."

Mark 16:17 AMP - "These signs will accompany those who have believed: in My name they will cast out demons, they will speak in new tongues."

Luke 11:13 AMP - "If you, then, being evil [that is, sinful by nature], know how to give good gifts to your children, how much more will your heavenly Father give the Holy Spirit to those who ask and continue to ask Him!"

Luke 24:49 NKJV - "Behold, I send the Promise of My Father upon you; but tarry in the city of Jerusalem until you are endued with power from on high."

Acts 2:4 AMP - "And they were all filled [that is, diffused throughout their being] with the Holy Spirit and began to speak in other tongues (different languages), as the Spirit was giving them the ability to speak out [clearly and appropriately]."

Acts 3:19 NKJV "Repent therefore and be converted, that your sins may be blotted out, so that times of refreshing may come from the presence of the Lord."

Acts 4:12 NKJV - "Nor is there salvation in any other, for there is no other name under heaven given among men by which we must be saved."

Romans 10:9 NKJV - "That if you confess with your mouth the Lord Jesus and believe in your heart that God has raised Him from the dead, you will be saved."

Romans 10:13 AMP - "For 'whoever calls on the name of the LORD [in prayer] will be saved.'"

Romans 12:1 AMP - "Therefore I urge you, brothers and sisters, by the mercies of God, to present your bodies [dedicating all of yourselves, set apart] as a living sacrifice, holy and well-pleasing to God, which is your rational (logical, intelligent) act of worship."

Romans 15:13 NKJV - "Now may the God of hope fill you with all joy and peace in believing, that you may abound in hope by the power of the Holy Spirit."

1 Corinthians 6:19-20 NKJV - "Or do you not know that your body is the temple of the Holy Spirit who is in you, whom you have from God, and you are not your own? For you were bought at a price; therefore glorify God in your body and in your spirit, which are God's."

2 Corinthians 4:4 NKJV - "Whose minds the god of this age has blinded, who do not believe, lest the light of the gospel of the glory of Christ, who is the image of God, should shine on them."

2 Corinthians 10:4-5 AMP - "The weapons of our warfare are not physical [weapons of flesh and blood]. Our weapons are divinely powerful for the destruction of fortresses. We are destroying sophisticated arguments and every exalted and proud thing that sets itself up against the [true] knowledge of God, and we are taking every thought and purpose captive to the obedience of Christ."

Galatians 3:13-14 NKJV - "Christ has redeemed us from the curse of the law, having become a curse for us (for it is written, 'Cursed is everyone who hangs on a tree'), that the blessing of Abraham might come upon the Gentiles in Christ Jesus, that we might receive the promise of the Spirit through faith."

Galatians 5:22-23 AMP - "But the fruit of the Spirit [the result of His presence within us] is love [unselfish concern for others], joy, [inner] peace, patience [not the ability to wait, but how we act while waiting], kindness, goodness, faithfulness, gentleness, self-control. Against such things there is no law."

Ephesians 6:14-18 NKJV - "Stand therefore, having girded your waist with truth, having put on the breastplate of righteousness, and having shod your feet with the preparation of the gospel of peace; above all, taking the shield of faith with which you will be able to quench all the fiery darts of the wicked one. And take the helmet of salvation, and the sword of the Spirit, which is the word of God; praying always with all prayer and supplication in the Spirit, being watchful to this end with all perseverance and supplication for all the saints."
Philippians 1:6 AMP "I am convinced and confident of this very thing, that He who has begun a good work in you will [continue to] perfect and complete it until the day of Christ Jesus [the time of His return]."

Philippians 4:8 AMP - "Finally, believers, whatever is true, whatever is honorable and worthy of respect, whatever is right and confirmed by God's word, whatever is pure and wholesome, whatever is lovely and brings peace, whatever is admirable and of good repute; if there is any excellence, if there is anything worthy of praise, think continually on these things [center your mind on them, and implant them in your heart]."

Philippians 4:19 NKJV - "And my God shall supply all your need according to His riches in glory by Christ Jesus."

James 1:17 NKJV - "Every good gift and every perfect gift is from above, and comes down from the Father of lights, with whom there is no variation or shadow of turning."

James 1:27 NKJV - "Pure and undefiled religion before God and the Father is this: to visit orphans and widows in their trouble, and to keep oneself unspotted from the world."

James 5:14 AMP - "Is anyone among you sick? He must call for the elders (spiritual leaders) of the church and they are to pray over him, anointing him with oil in the name of the Lord."

1 John 1:7 NKJV - "But if we walk in the light as He is in the light, we have fellowship with one another, and the blood of Jesus Christ His Son cleanses us from all sin."

1 John 1:9 NKJV - "If we confess our sins, He is faithful and just to forgive us our sins and to cleanse us from all unrighteousness."

1 John 2:27 AMP - "As for you, the anointing [the special gift, the preparation] which you received from Him remains [permanently] in you, and you have no need for anyone to teach you. But just as His anointing teaches you [giving you insight through the presence of the Holy Spirit] about all things, and is true and is not a lie, and just as His anointing has taught you, you must remain in Him [being rooted in Him, knit to Him]."

1 John 4:4 AMP - "Little children (believers, dear ones), you are of God, and you belong to Him and have [already] overcome them [the agents of the antichrist]; because He who is in you is greater than he (Satan) who is in the world [of sinful mankind]."

2 Peter 3:18 NKJV - "But grow in the grace and knowledge of our Lord and Savior Jesus Christ. To Him be the glory both now and forever. Amen."

www.ingramcontent.com/pod-product-compliance
Lightning Source LLC
Chambersburg PA
CBHW042121100526
44587CB00025B/4138